The Power of Loving Yourself

15 successful tools you can use to change the way you look at yourself and the world around you

All love starts with self-love, yet many of us are trained to believe that self-love is selfish and narcissistic. We push away compliments. We reject positive thoughts about who we are, how we look, what we have achieved and what we are achieving.

In her amazing Itty Bitty™ Book, Jade Elizabeth teaches how to become a healthy, happy self-loving you – a person who exudes energy, happiness, caring, joy and confidence. You will love this book!

Some Questions This Book Addresses:

- Why is receiving just as important as giving?
- How do I sabotage myself and how can I stop?
- How do I create a better understanding of what perfection does to me?

If you are ready to invest in changing your life, pick up a copy of this powerful book today and experience the joy and success that come with loving yourself.

Your Amazing
Itty Bitty™

Self-Esteem Book

*15 Essential Steps for Gaining and Keeping
High Self-Worth*

Jade Elizabeth

Published by Itty Bitty™ Publishing
A subsidiary of S & P Productions, Inc.

Printed in the United States of America

Itty Bitty™ Publishing
311 Main Street, Suite E
El Segundo, CA 90245
(310) 640-8885

ISBN: 978-1-931191-85-2

I would like to thank my husband, Ralph, for all his support through my healing journey. I would also like to thank Catherine Morris for her years of friendship and all the wisdom she shared with me over the years; for helping me learn how to listen to my own intuition and teaching me many of the skills I teach today. I would like to thank Robin Duncan for bringing me back to my Spiritual Source through A Course in Miracles. She showed me a new way to look at God. To Jay Williams who taught me NLP and how to release the old limiting beliefs – thank you. Your loving and caring way allowed me to learn and heal at the same time. I would like to thank Joan Meijer and Suzy Prudden, the publishers of Itty Bitty™ Books, for without them, this book would not have been possible.

I consider each one a mentor who has greatly supported me on my journey over the years. Without their help and support, I would not be the person I am today. So again, thank you for all you have given me.

Stop by our Itty Bitty™ website to find
interesting blog entries regarding self-love.

www.IttyBittyPublishing.com

Or visit Jade Elizabeth at:

www.JadeElizabeth.com

Table of Contents

Introduction

In this Itty Bitty™ Book you will find 15 essential things you can do to know your self-worth. Each step will change the way you look at yourself and the world around you. All you need to do is choose a new and different way of observing and judging and the rest will be history.

This was the process I used to take me from a place of self-sabotage to a place of loving and believing in myself.

You can accomplish anything you set your mind to. The only secret is you must choose to.

Step 1
Aware of Your Own Self-Talk

Your self-talk is the private conversation you have with yourself inside your head. It reflects the positive or negative beliefs you hold. You discover those beliefs by listening to the way you talk to yourself and by looking at your results. Positive beliefs have positive outcomes. Negative beliefs have negative outcomes.

1. It is important to pay attention to your inner voice and the results that replay over and over in your life. You cannot change something until you become *aware* of it.
2. Negative beliefs could sound like: "I am not smart enough to do that job."
3. Positive beliefs could look as simple as always finding a parking spot when you need one.
4. Negative beliefs could look like going out for job after job and only landing low-paying positions.
5. Start to notice when the bad and the good self-talk shows up, with each manifesting exactly what you were attempting to do.
6. Start to notice the patterns of the unwanted results in your life.

The Process of Becoming Aware

- Begin to pay attention to your words and thoughts – even sarcastic sighs can be informative.
- Start a log or journal of your negative self-talk.
- Questions you could ask yourself: What did I want to do, say or accomplish before my negative self-talk started? Jot it down.
- Notice if you evaluate or judge your actions or decisions on a regular basis? If so; what, when and how often? Jot it down.
- Your log or journal is the start of your internal roadmap. In order to understand and make changes, it is important to have a written account so you can begin to get a clear picture of your negative beliefs.
- Your *awareness* will assist you in taking the first step to change.

Step 2
How Do I Sabotage Myself?

What you believe – what you tell yourself – you will create. Every 10 seconds you make a choice. Statistics show that 20% of your choices are conscious. The other 80% are automatic and made by your subconscious mind.

1. Ask yourself whether you consistently play to your highest and best purpose or whether you play to your limitations.
2. When you are making a decision based on something that happened in the past, you are not making a conscious choice because your past is dictating your present moment. For example, "I tried that once before and it ended badly."
3. When you desire to do something new and your self-talk tells you it wouldn't work, you won't succeed or you will look silly and give up before you start or quit before you succeed (usually just before you succeed). That is your subconscious programming at work.
4. You sabotage yourself by allowing the negative self-talk to run your life and the actions you take.

You Will Always Be *RIGHT*!

- The universal Law of Attraction states, "whatever you think, feel or believe will come to you."
- Your thoughts are like magnets.
  - If you are thinking in lack you will see more lack.
  - If you believe you can't do something, you won't.
  - If you believe it will end badly, it will.
  - *You are always right!*

Today start a new habit.
- Every time you become *aware* of saying to yourself, "I can't," imagine erasing it off your whiteboard and replacing it with "I can!" This will shift the energy.
- Avoid saying "I will." That puts whatever it is into the future and delays it happening.
- Every time you change a limiting thought to something that could be true it will stop the self-sabotage before it takes hold.
- The more you do this, the easier it will get. It only takes practice and becoming *aware*.

Step 3
Belief in What Other People Say

You have been taught to respect and believe what your parents, teachers and authority figures tell you. All these people share what they have been taught or what their beliefs are, even if they are not right for you.

1. What if your mom or dad believed you had to work hard for your money? How do you think that would affect you? That belief will lead you to jobs where you must work hard. Jobs you might love would not be on your radar.

2. Most doctors are taught to look for what can be fixed. This means they will find something to fix because that is what they are looking for, especially if you come in not feeling well.

3. Teachers teach you what is written in books or they teach what they know (their beliefs and opinions). Does that mean they are correct?

4. People can say hurtful things to you. Does that mean they know what they are talking about?

Before you accept other people's beliefs and statements make certain you agree with them no matter which authority is doing the talking.

What Others Say Has Nothing To Do With You.

- When someone tells you:
    - You're stupid!
    - You'll never amount to anything!
    - You can't do that!   Or
    - You must work hard for your money!
- What they are really saying is *they* can't. They don't believe in themselves and they are projecting their limitations on you. Or, they don't want you to succeed because you threaten their fragile sense of security.
- People often get upset when you don't agree with them or do it their way. Why? Because we were taught only one of us can be right. If you do it your way, you must be wrong.
- People who believe they are not good enough lash out at others because it helps them feel more powerful.
- Most bullies do not have good self-esteem. So to make themselves feel worthy, they lash out.
- Next time someone says something that is not loving or empowering, STOP LISTENING.

Now, tell yourself, *I am a being of light and love, worthy of respect*. Keep repeating this to yourself until you feel better. Notice the energy shift within you.

Step 4
Affirmations

You may have been told how important affirmations are. Well, there is a good side and a not-so-good side to affirmations.

1.   Affirmations are a way to change a limiting belief.
2.   You must be in harmony with the words you say.
3.   If the affirmation brings up bad internal self-talk, don't say it. You will be defeating the purpose.
4.   The smaller and gentler the affirmations, the easier it is for you to feel good when you say them.
5.   Your affirmations could look like:
     a.   Today I appreciate myself *a little more* than yesterday!
     b.   Today I am *willing* to love myself more than I did yesterday!
     c.   Today is filled with the possibility of miracles!
     d.   I now allow myself to achieve success in any area I apply myself!
6.   Write your affirmations on your bathroom mirror with a dry eraser pen.

Being in Alignment with Your Words and Emotions Is The #1 Key

- The most important thing is feeling good when you say your affirmations because that good feeling is what starts the process of change.
- When your words and emotions match you will get the most out of the affirmation. You will begin to experience how powerful your words are.
- You start to experience more confidence in what you are doing and saying when that happens.
- Use words in your affirmation like:
  - I'm willing to…
  - I allow…
  - I encourage myself to…
  - It's ok to receive…
- Any of the above words included in an affirmation will take out the resistance. Remember when there is no resistance, success is achieved.
- Take time to create a strong positive emotion as you say your affirmations, either out loud or in your mind.
- When saying your affirmations in the mirror, look deep into your own eyes, the same way you look at someone when giving a compliment.
- The more effort and attention you give to your affirmations, the quicker your success.

Step 5
Complaining & Judging

When you complain or judge, you keep yourself in a negative frame of mind. It's like having your feet stuck in mud and you can't move. Complaining is actually a negative affirmation.

1. Pay attention to how much you complain and what you complain about.
2. Notice what you are judging and see if it matches what you feel judged about.
3. Your complaining and judging will keep you in a bad mood and continue a downward spiral of more negativity. You get what you give.
4. The next time you complain or judge something or someone, tune into your physical body and notice how you feel.
   a. Are your shoulders tight?
   b. Do you feel like you have a pit in your stomach?
   c. Or, something else?
5. Once you become aware of how your body responds your negative thoughts and statements, you make different choices. The better your choices the better you will feel.

Important Reasons for Shifting Your Thought Patterns

- When your mind goes into complaining mode, your body becomes stressed.
- Judging others will cause you to judge yourself even more. (The mind does not hear the words you, he she, it, them. When you judge others, the mind takes the judgment on as something negative about yourself.)
- The more you complain, the more you will have to complain about.
- Begin to look for something good in yourself and others, no matter how small. This will start you moving in a positive direction.
- Get in the habit of stopping yourself when you notice you're complaining; pretend you are erasing it off a white board in your head and then find something positive to replace it with. Go to the affirmations you wrote in Step 4 and say them out loud.
- Taking small steps will make enormous changes over time. You just have to take the first step.

Step 6
Controlling Your Emotions

This is one of the most important steps because it will keep you from sabotaging yourself. It is often the case for everyone to jump too quickly to a decision when their emotions are high.

1. If you feel bad, ask yourself the question, "What can I do right now to change this?" This will start your unconscious mind working to give you more choices.
2. Your emotions can take you places you don't want to go. So before you react to something someone said or did, *STOP,* and take a few breaths before you speak.
3. Runaway emotions will also spiral you in a downward direction that is very hard to stop.
4. When your thoughts go to self criticizing, your emotions will go on high alert. This can start an emotional loop that can be hard to stop.

Your Emotions Will Override Your Thoughts

- When you are thrown into a downward spiral, as soon as you can, take out some paper and a pen and start to write all the bad feelings onto the paper. This is called dumping.
- Getting the emotions out of your body and conscious mind is important for your overall health.
- Every time you notice yourself feeling bad, use the dumping technique. This will keep you from lashing out at family and friends or just holding it in.
- Holding negative emotions in will cause you to become sick over time.
- Another method is to go hug a tree. Wrap your arms around the tree and imagine all the negative emotions are flowing into the tree. Sounds funny, but it works.

Step 7
Have a Positive Attitude about Yourself

Your attitude and beliefs about yourself are very important because you will always be right. It is a universal law. This is why your list "*The things I like about myself*" is so important.

1. Always have your list handy so, when you become aware of something you like about yourself, you can jot it down.
2. Pay attention to all the good things others say about you and write them down on your list as well.
3. Create some positive thoughts when you arise in the morning, such as:
   a. Today is filled with miracles!
   b. Today is more powerful and positive than yesterday!
   c. I am grateful for this day!
   d. I am filled with light!
   e. I am unique and that is a wonderful thing!
4. Use your imagination when you create your positive thought. For example, as you say, I am filled with light; begin to experience yourself filling with light. Then stop and notice the difference.

Your Personal Attitude Will Shift the Energy You Transmit

- When people say good things about you, this will give you a broader perspective. Tell yourself, "Wow, that's me they're talking about!"
- The more attention you give to your positive thoughts, the more you will experience the things you want.
- If something comes up that you don't like, *STOP* and begin to focus on what you do want.
- State one of your affirmations or start to read the good things on your list of *"The things I like about myself."* Any of these will help you.
- Remember, you are the only one who can do this. You don't have to make big leaps, just one small step at a time. The more small steps you make, the easier it is, and over time the small steps will make a big impact in your life. I know because I've been there!

Step 8
Receiving and Giving

Receiving is one of the main ingredients for achieving self-esteem. The problem is, most people have difficulty allowing themselves to receive.

1. When someone gives you a compliment, *STOP* – and just say thank you! In your mind, don't start saying bad things about the compliment. Just allow yourself to fully receive what was said.
2. Receiving is one of the most powerful gifts you can give yourself. It shows you believe you're important. For example:
   a. When someone hugs you or shakes your hand, do you only pay attention to giving or do you allow yourself to receive their hug or handshake as well?
   b. When someone gives you a complement, do you fully receive it or do you blush and dismiss it?
3. When you allow yourself to feel and receive love, you will have more to give and share with others.
4. Giving is a wonderful thing. Receiving is a *must* for self-love.

Allowing Yourself to Receive is the First Big Step to Improving Self-Worth

- When you allow yourself to receive, you make the person doing the giving, happy.
- When you fill yourself with love first, you give from the overflow. This allows you to have more to give.
- If all you do is give, you will eventually have burn-out.
- Giving is a way of sharing. Receiving is opening up and allowing a gift in.
- The true meaning of giving is – give with an open heart and nothing to gain other than it makes you feel good. Don't even expect a thank you!
- Tell yourself every day, "It's OK for me to receive my dreams and wishes."
- By allowing yourself to receive, you show the Universe/Divine Source you are ready to receive even more.

Step 9
Breaking the Chains of Old Programming

Step 1 helped you become aware of your self-talk; now it's time to take the next step – ACTION.

1. Start to focus on what you want, not what you see. What you see is yesterday's thoughts.
2. Pay attention to the things you are good at and like about yourself.
3. Start doing things that bring you joy and happiness. Maybe a walk on the beach, a walk in the park or something as simple as reading a good book.
4. When you think a negative thought, stop yourself and think of something you are good at. If you really want change, you must do this; no one else can do it for you.

The Importance of Paying Attention

- You are the only one in charge of you. So make your thoughts count.
- By focusing on what you want, the Universe begins to work out the details to bring it to you.
- The more you stay in the "poor me" pattern or in a bad mood, the worse it will get. It's up to you, so decide you are worth it – because you are.
- Start each day with an affirmation such as, "I am worthy of receiving my dreams."

Step 10
Gratitude for What You Have

One of the biggest secrets for self-love is the vibrational energy of gratitude because the only thing more powerful is love.

1. When you have gratitude for the things you already have, you will begin to receive more. That is how the Law of Attraction works.
2. Begin a gratitude routine. It should look like this:
   a. Every morning think of 5 to 10 new things you're grateful for, such as: I love the color of the wallpaper/paint, because it makes me happy.
   b. In the evening as you sit on the edge of the bed, think about your day and only the wonderful things that happened. Then give gratitude for the best one. Let the feeling of gratitude fill you as you lay your head down to sleep.
3. Name everything you can think of about yourself you are grateful for, such as: I love my smile because it makes me feel good inside to smile.

Small Things Are Important Too

Here are some examples that will help you to start thinking about how you want to express your gratitude.

- I am grateful for _____ ...
  - My eyes because...
  - My flower garden because...
  - The color of my bedroom because...
  - For all the builders that took part in building my house/apartment because...
  - For the farmers that grew the food at the market because...
  - For fresh drinking water because...
- Once you start your gratitude routine, start to pay attention to how different things are and how different you feel.

Step 11
Perfectionism

An almost sure-fire way to set yourself up for failure is to judge everything you do with the goal of such perfection that there is no possible way for you to achieve it.

1. Striving to do the best you can is a powerful thing as long as you don't judge how perfect it is. It is ok to look at what you did and see if there is anything you could do better. Just don't judge it wrong, simply because it can be improved.
2. You can always find a better way to do something once it's done. That doesn't mean the original way wasn't good or even great.
3. Sometimes we strive to do a perfect job because other people will give us a thumbs up.
4. Notice that when you care, you always try to do a much better job. This is usually when you judge yourself more harshly – and that is when you need to lighten up on yourself and acknowledge the good job you did.

Nothing in the World Is Perfect

- Sit for a moment and think of what perfect is for you. If it means nothing can be improved, you will never achieve it because there will always be a better way.
- Start to look in nature and realize that nothing is really perfect.
- Look at a tree and notice how beautiful it is. Now notice all the imperfections in it. Ask yourself, "Does it take away from the beauty? No."

Step 12
Using the Mirror

Mirror work is one of the most powerful processes you can do to love yourself because it is seeing you, telling you, how good you are.

1. Look in the mirror, into your eyes, and talk to yourself. Start with easy things, such as, "I like you!" or "I like your smile." In the beginning, the simpler the statement, the better.
2. Every day, look in the mirror and say only positive things to yourself.
3. Having a conversation with yourself in a mirror can change the way you feel about yourself and bring you clarity.
4. Instead of believing your self-talk, look at yourself and tell yourself what you want to hear. Even if you don't believe it at first, watching yourself say it is powerful.

Mirror, Mirror – What I See

- When you look in the mirror, into your own eyes, you are talking to your soul.
- The mirror creates a space for you to begin to believe in yourself.
- It is a way to say nice things to yourself, instead of listening to the negative mind chatter.
- Take your affirmations from Step #4 and say them while looking at yourself in the mirror.
- Look at your reflection in the mirror and after each affirmation smile, so you can see yourself smiling back at you.
- Ask yourself what you are willing to do to bring your dreams into reality.

Step 13
Take Control of Your Thoughts

Your thoughts are a key component to feeling empowered. When you direct your thoughts to what you want instead of what you see, you will begin to change everything, because only you can make the change. No one else can do it for you.

1. Your past thoughts create what you see, so imagine what you would like to see.
2. People can not show up any different than what you expect. If you expect them to be rude, they will be rude. If you expect them to kind, they will be kind.
3. In the morning, take a few minutes to plan your day. Either write it down or get a clear picture of what you would like to see. Important: make it attainable!
4. Your unconscious mind is symbolic and does not process negative words such as, 'no,' 'don't,' 'can't,' etc. For example, "I don't want to be sick." What your unconscious mind understands is want and sick.
5. The key is to focus on ONLY what you want, not what you don't want.
6. How you treat yourself is how you are inviting the world to treat you.

Your Thoughts Are Powerful

- Learn to focus your thoughts on what you want.
- Always start and end your day with powerful positive thoughts.
- Put Post-it® notes all around your house and carry some in your wallet with affirmations such as:
    - I was born unlimited!
    - My desires and wishes come to me easily!
    - I am open *NOW* to receive _! (fill in the blank)
- The more positive your thoughts, the more joy, happiness and abundance you bring to yourself. Remember the negative words the unconscious mind doesn't hear. So keep it simple and positive.

Step 14
The Power to Trust Yourself

When you start to trust your decisions and choices, you are on the right road to happiness. Trusting is a good thing, trusting yourself is a powerful tool for healing.

1. Start to notice how many times you have to do something before you trust your decisions. Is it three, four – or maybe more?
2. Start to do little things that you believe you can do successfully because this will give you confidence to do more.
3. It is not selfish to do what is best for you, no matter what anyone says.
4. Each time you trust your intuition and go for it, you are moving in the right direction.

You Need To Be #1

- Not everyone will like you and that's OK, because you don't like everybody you know.
- Surround yourself with people who empower you.
- If you get a bad feeling about someone, you are probably right. Trust it!
- The more you start to trust yourself, the more others will do the same.

Step 15
Belief in a Higher Power

Your belief in something greater than you is imperative, because it moves you from limitation to hope.

1. It is important to ask for what you want. Most people think the God/Source knows what that is.
2. Your beliefs and past experience is what creates how you see yourself. Today, accept the truth that you were created whole and perfect.
3. The more faith and trust you have that a higher power is here for you, the more you will witness it.
4. Make the choice to know that it is done the moment you ask.
5. Believe that whatever you ask for is already waiting for you. No matter what your past experiences were, know it will show up as soon as you are in alignment with it.

Ask — Trust — Receive

- Always ask for what you want.
- When you ask, follow with, "I want it because..."
- You don't have to know how. You don't have to control it. Just let go and trust.
- Now allow yourself to completely receive and know you deserve it.
- Know that God/Source believes in you, so it's time you do the same.

You've finished. Before you go...

<u>Tweet/share that you finished this book.</u>

Please star rate this book.

Reviews are solid gold to writers. Please take a few minutes to give us some itty bitty feedback on this book.

ABOUT THE AUTHOR

Jade Elizabeth started out like many people, with no self-esteem or self-worth. She believed she was the only one who felt that way. One day she read a book that changed everything. She realized for the first time she had to start loving herself for who she was and not look to others for validation. This took her on a journey of self-discovery and years of study and healing.

Her credentials are: Intuitive Healer; Reiki Master/Teacher; Hypnotherapist; Master in Neuro-Linguistic Programming (NLP); T.I.M.E. techniques; and Emotional Freedom Techniques (EFT).

As she began to heal, her thoughts were to share her information and assist others who wanted to feel love for themselves.

Her passion is to motivate, educate and inspire Self-Love!

www.JadeElizabeth.com

**If you liked this Itty Bitty Book
You Might also enjoy...**

- **Your Amazing Itty Bitty™ Gratitude Book** – Belinda Lee Cook

- **Your Amazing Itty Bitty™ Book of Empowerment Through Hope** – LeAnna Blackmon

- **Your Amazing Itty Bitty™ Astrology Book** – Carol Pilkington

And many other Amazing Itty Bitty™ books

Made in the USA
San Bernardino, CA
30 January 2016